Bed of Impatiens

Has American poetry ever produced a fresher, savvier, grittier, more elegant, and drop-dead formally exhilarating sequence than Katie Hartsock's "Hotels, Motels, and Extended Stays"? If so, I've yet to see it. Hartsock is as deft (and loving) with the vulgarities of truck stop rent-by-the-hour as with the secret wit of rhyme, or the venerables of Homeric epic: her range and her inventiveness appear to know no limit. And this is just a fraction of what bursts to life in *Bed of Impatiens*. I'm dazzled by the sheer bounty of it.

—Linda Gregerson, author of *Prodigal:*
New and Selected Poems, 1976 to 2014

Like René Magritte I want to paint "This is not a first book" under this first book. It is Lolita all grown up and taking us on a cross-country tour of the motels she stayed in with Humbert. It's St. Augustine as Dennis Rodman, elbowing us out of position underneath God's basket. But it's not a cacophony of surrealism. Ms. Hartsock's classical training—her knowledge and powerful rhythms—is the ground, the spine of this book (pun intended); but the excitement is watching the ancient and the contemporary meet in an explosion of true Form. This is generous, tough-minded, yet tender work, where the ghosts of the past have to prove their worth in a contemporary mind full of love, sex, Youngstown, the spirit, wild papyri, the Karamazovs' unacknowledged sister, Mr. Vodka, the Ohio and Mississippi River valleys, Molly Bloom, grubbiness, men. Just for starters. It's a wild (and exhilarating) ride of language and smarts, this first book that's not a first book.

—James Cummins, author of *Still Some Cake*

Katie Hartsock's book of poems *Bed of Impatiens* is, for a first volume, unusually broad in its range and fierce in its attitudes. Although her title suggests a pretty pastoral, that is not where her taste leads her. Instead, her characteristic vantage includes landscapes derelict and macabre, like the flooded grave in the first poem, and the endless highways of the US, with their extended-stay motels and the ghosts that inhabit them. For such American locales, it is a marvel that the poet makes room for a sequence of poems devoted to the anguish of the early Christian memoirist Saint Augustine, and that a gloss on the hero's homecoming in the *Odyssey* hinges on the epiphany of mutual irritation through which Odysseus and his wife recognize and salute each other. Hartsock is a sharp and clever reader of the books of nature and of art, yet writes in nobody's shadow.

—Mary Kinzie, author of *California Sorrow*

What truth to find in a world whose rivers "we cannot swim in and no/ cannot drink the water/ cannot imagine that," a land of "seedless sweetness" and dank motels that are its monuments to transience? Katie Hartsock's answer in her ambitious first collection, *Bed of Impatiens,* is to wander and "let the weather in," to keep recalibrating her position in an ever-shifting poetic landscape. Pythagoras, Emily Dickinson, and Tom Petty converge on a Chicago lakeside street where the speaker both is and is not present; Euripidean slave women provide the chorus for her return to the "murk-loving waters" of a ghosted Mississippi; motel rooms strangers have "shared separately" proliferate hilariously, populated with paradox and loss. A beautiful, formally inventive verse rendering of Saint Augustine's *Confessions,* alternating with first-person poems of earthly love, constitutes the book's final section. "I have felt the bliss," Hartsock testifies, ever the truth-seeker, ever the denier, "and the burning too."

—Lee Sharkey, author of *Calendars of Fire*

BED *of* IMPATIENS

POEMS BY
Katie Hartsock

ABLE MUSE PRESS

Able Muse Press

www.ablemusepress.com

Printed in the United States of America

Library of Congress Control Number: 2015955767

ISBN 978-1-927409-65-7 (paperback)
ISBN 978-1-927409-66-4 (digital)

Cover image: "Night Discovery" by Alexander Pepple
(with "Dragon on the Red Impatiens" by Jim Persons)

Cover & book design by Alexander Pepple

Able Muse Press is an imprint of *Able Muse: A Review of Poetry, Prose & Art*—at
www.ablemuse.com

Able Muse Press
467 Saratoga Avenue #602
San Jose, CA 95129

for my mother, Mary Ann

Acknowledgments

I am grateful to the editors of the following journals where many of the poems in this collection originally appeared, sometimes in earlier versions:

Arion: "Myrmidons" and "Crazy"

Beloit Poetry Journal: "The Buried in Sleep and Wine Hotel," "The Grant Me the Stamina to Pray Extended Stay Motel," and "The Western Edge of a Time Zone Hotel"

Birmingham Poetry Review: "Augustine I," "Augustine III," "Augustine V," "Augustine VI," "Augustine VII," "Augustine VIII," "Augustine XI," and "Augustine XIII"

Crab Orchard Review: "Western Reserve"

DIAGRAM: "The Ducks on a Whiskey River Motel"

Down to the Dark River: Poems about the Mississippi River (Louisiana Literature Press, 2015): *"Veritas Caput"* and "Mississippi Stasimon"

Fifth Wednesday: "Medea in Red River Gorge" and "The Angelization of Mr. Vodka"

Hanging Loose: "Mimesis"

H_NGM_N: "The Bump on a Log Hotel" and "The I'm Not as Good as I Once Was, but I'm as Good Once as I Ever Was Motel"

Iron Horse Literary Review: "Onion"

Jet Fuel Review: "The Let's Have a Cigarette and Assess the Situation Extended Stay Motel" and "N67: Stella Maris"

Massachusetts Review: "Midnight Mass"

Matter Journal: "Highway 101"

Measure: "The Flooded Grave"

Michigan Quarterly Review: "The Natural Look" and "The Sister Karamazov"

Midwestern Gothic: "My Labor, and My Leisure Too"

RHINO: "On the Heat of Upstate Travel in the Advancing Polar Air" and Cuticles"

Southern Indiana Review: "Wings on Wheels" and "Bonfire"

Southwest Review: "The Demolition Derby Motel" and "The Philoctetes Extended Stay Hotel"

wicked alice: "The Things Will Never Be the Same Extended Stay Hotel," "The Drop-Kick Me Sweet Jesus through the Goalposts of Life Motel," "Route 6: Balmers Herberge," and "The Only Living Girl in Chicago Extended Stay Hotel"

Fourteen poems from the second section were included as a chapbook, *Hotels, Motels, and Extended Stays,* in the 2014 Quartet Series collection *A Good Wall,* published by Toadlily Press, Chappaqua, New York.

"Veritas Caput" was published as a limited-edition chapbook by Passim Editions in 2015.

I would also like to thank the Helen Zell Writers' Program and the Hopwood Program at the University of Michigan, and the Eastern Frontier Education Association on Norton Island, Maine. For your spirit, support, friendship, and feedback, thank you: T Hetzel, Holly Virginia Clark, Jacob

Saenz, Brian Bouldrey, Laura Passin, Thomas Lynch, Francesca Tataranni, Ruth Martin Curry, Helen Polowy, Lee Sharkey, Marianne Hopman, Betsy Erkkila, Reginald Gibbons, John Wynne, Laura Kasischke, Linda Gregerson, Lorna Goodison, Jonathan Kamholtz, Amanda Cadogan, Carol Eding, Hank Scotch, Adria Forte, Katie Kemme, James Cummins, Brian Yates, Sean Duffy, Darci Cooper, Amelia Jarret, Jessica Wright, David and Deborah Geltner, Dave Hartsock, Walter David Hartsock, Mary Ann Hartsock, and, especially, Jonathan Geltner.

Foreword

KATIE HARTSOCK IS ATTRACTED to "beauty in otherwise unlovely places," and even the beauty of what might seem ugly. In an interview, she has recalled looking around in autumn in Youngstown, where she grew up, and hearing someone say, "It's nice here this time of year, because of the rust." Many poetry readers may think that the beauty of our wounded world is a topic that has been displaced by sheer quantities of suffering, but also, in poems, by irony, a dislike or distrust of meaning and other poetic fashions of affect. But Hartsock finds something beautiful where it's not expected, and outside the usual expectations of what beauty is, and also finds it in what might seem to others unbeautiful, like that post-industrial Midwestern rust. She has a broad view of beauty and a long view of the human spirit.

Hartsock writes with skill and seriousness and also with appealing intimacy and immediacy, both when in a mood of deep spirit and when lighthearted. And behind these qualities there is her clearly evident love of poetry, which she has fed with a tremendous scope of reading, from ancient Greek to the poems of the day before yesterday. Her book interleaves many sorts of scenes and things and moments—from the margins of our contemporary US (in her poems set in hotels and motels with amusingly improbable, and mostly odd but perfectly apt names), to the ancient Greek and Roman worlds. To the latter she alludes, throughout this first book that I welcome for its beautiful rust and unrushed beauty.

She combines both ancient and contemporary in her sequence of poems drawn from or created out of Augustine's still luminous *Confessions*. Her formal inventiveness is pleasing (as in "Ayr"); her juxtapositions are delightful:

> Pythagoras
> had a golden thigh, some disciples said,
>   and could be in two places at once;
>   there, with the dunes and roofs and bricks
>   and brunettes of Michigan,
>   and here on the street I crossed diagonally,
>   calling out his name.
>   ("My Labor, and My Leisure Too")

Her sometimes startling insight into the ordinary gives us that small blessed thrill of the compact, eloquently inventive, poetic line: on a cold day outside, the poetic self leans toward her lover . . . "and with my wordless tongue/ I eat your breath" ("Si Quaeris"). She ranges from the amusing wit of "The Angelization of Mr. Vodka" all the way to her ventriloquizing, in thirteen of the poems of the sequence that is the third part of *Bed of Impatiens,* of St. Augustine:

> Theatergoers, we were the theater—
> the sighs I heaved from my seat, enraptured,
> were no far cry from those in lovers' arms,
> false love as cathartic as tragedies.
>
> The Carthaginian I've still in me
> exquisitely thrills, weeps to tell these tales;
> I keep a snuffer close by his candle.

I want to praise the pleasures of Hartsock's language. She can move her thinking by moving from sound to sound—here, from "cathartic" to "Carthaginian"—and she can move a sound to show more of the thought that's already in that sound (<u>barefac</u>ed . . . <u>beard</u>less . . . <u>beggar</u>"): "My barefaced panegyrics for the beardless boy emperor/ were goading me—frenetic I paced Milan, past a beggar/ drunk at noon" ("Augustine VI").

She provides many pleasures of sound and sense holding hands as they dance: the phrase "in a mass of peasants at the monastery" seems to turn the "*mass*" into the "*monastery*"—one of those poetic magic tricks that produce a truth rather than an illusion. Another: "the *full*ness of its *futil*ity." Another, beginning with Augustine's Latin: "*Deus meus,* dear muse my God."

So in Hartsock's poems there's often a restoration of a sense of language as our way of sometimes, yes, finding our way to something, not always falling short of it. Something that may be delicately balanced, easily toppled, but for its moment, has the sense and sound of an elusive, valuable meaning in it. And in her poems we can hear that poetry mustn't remove pleasure from itself. Even in the falling short of saying what one wishes one could think of, and could think of how to say, there can be the truth of the effort of articulating. One can hear it in these poems.

An often amused and good-hearted spirit sets the tone of some of Hartsock's poems, but the long historical and literary view of this poet also encompasses the tragic. Her use—sometimes jesting, sometimes sober—of classical antiquity gives us a sense that each life can be seen as part of the continuity of human experience; this enlarges us as we—as individual selves but also somehow representative beings too—live again the love and sorrow that others have lived. This is one of the things that poems could bring to readers thousands of years ago and still bring us today. Even in Hartsock's sequence of imagined "Hotels, Motels and Extended Stays," it's against the background of her long view that her present-day scenes and reflections are set: "There is no pain like knowing the polis/ is doomed." (Note the nifty double syntax created by that line-break.) And also, in a motel, in "I-80: Liberty Inn," the thought comes that Odysseus

... did not expect, so could not resist,
the promise of the Sirens' song:

not sex but knowledge,
intimate with the war,
what each man was to that war.

Odysseus's rowers, whose ears were stopped with beeswax, could not hear, and suffered no torment of temptation; but in the motel what comes to mind, when thinking about him and perhaps even hearing those Sirens, is that

We know the song, how
it puts on the hurt to meet the mouth
that sings. . . .

One of the great strengths of holding in mind—in a poem, especially—both the ancient and the present-day is that human longing and loss can be elevated a little, and sometimes even nearly hallowed, when set against the patterns of myth. A new poem reenacts this particular long-standing power of poetry, among its many others. Thus we may sometimes find the solace of significance in what otherwise might seem meaningless or might impose on us a meaning we can't bear. Speaking as Augustine, Hartsock sees God himself as "a mosaic of meanings,/ of differing truths that do not undo/ each other."

In the especially lovely poem, "Route 6: Balmers Herberge," on the road from one place to some other, pear trees in an orchard bring the feeling of . . . perhaps it's loneliness . . . around to this conclusion: "Abandoned, do not/ deny what you met."

Open to encounter, memory, feeling, avid for them, eloquent about them, these poems.

—Reginald Gibbons

Contents

One.

WILD PAPYRI

Two.

HOTELS, MOTELS, AND EXTENDED STAYS

Three.

impatiens: *an East African plant with abundant red, pink, or white flowers . . . ORIGIN late 18th century, from Latin, literally* **"impatient"** *(because the capsules of the plant readily burst open when touched).*
— New Oxford American Dictionary

One.

Certain papyrus fragments preserve verses of ancient texts that differ from the standardized versions. Because of these variations they are called "wild" or "eccentric" papyri.

"The Flooded Grave"

—After the light box by Jeff Wall
Art Institute of Chicago

Beside the shoveled mound of glebe,
a red-orange-yellow shoal
of starfish and anemones
dwells within the hole.
Far afield, a hose lies flat,
pointed at this pool
as if its shower gave the *fiat*
lux. Gravedigger tools
can resurrect, the burial
ground can learn to swim.
Walled in by earth, germs of tidal
foam still top the scrim
of cropped saltwater. Visions prove
how they live: they move.

The Sister Karamazov

For David

All things that occur in fours
have a fifth, a conspirator
unbeknownst to the conspiracy,
and ignored by the narrator.
A bastard season of a sister
who borrows the defining features
of her brothers: the cynic,
the sensualist, the wretch,
the mystic. Without her,
they cannot become each other.

An onlooker, she remains unintroduced
at a distance—across a potato cart
at market, a few stools down the bar,
pausing by the picture windows
of their quarters, on her knees and forehead
in a mass of peasants at the monastery—
fiercely adoring all four
now that they're all in town, not for long.

She wanders through them as she would a forest
and sees herself, a tree that grows there.

There are nights all five
roam the streets alone,
inquisitors born from a father
who cannot answer for anything.
The brothers turn disparate
corners, unaware, towards her:
the wheel around spokes,
the deck's forlorn joker,
apocryphal gospel,
quintessential wind.

Any direction steers her closer
to one brother and farther from another,
and farther from one brother and
closer to another.

Preternatal

Every navel orange, a clone
of mutant fruit from a single tree
grafted over centuries to

repeat its original accident:
sterile twins, conjoined at the head,
and the small one never finished

or vanished. Their seedless sweetness
quickly made them a favorite, soon
ships carried branches overseas

so I could split the segments of
this double, this delicious freaky
creature, almost sensual

in the fullness of its futility.
Some say Helen never went
to Troy, she sat her beauty down

by the undefiled banks of the Nile
and waited years. Her phantom twin,
made in and made of heaven's germs,

sailed off to start that war—all part
of some celestial downsize plan
targeting the too many humans

on earth, overburdened with our weight.
It worked. The vapor played her role,
all the sex as unreal as the deaths were vain,

and not one heir from the whole debacle,
for even heroes cannot get a cloud
with child. Who hasn't fallen

for a phantom, gone to bed and been
the only one really there?
I can't eat these oranges like I did,

pretending the miniature twin was a brain
I would take in a single bite to better
my own. You begin to desiccate

as I study the peel of your blossom end,
its flowery confusion of inner and outer:
imperfect double for not, I think,

just any navel, but a pregnant belly's
button, pushed out by its seed.
Your name becomes what you cannot

do, little graftling—conceive.
I bear that stamp of being fed
in the womb you happened to resemble.

Proverbial

If I could be a fuckin' fisherman I would.
—John Lennon

Flies whine outside the trash can, wanting in,
and the flies inside would die to get out.
The wall dividing us is only so thin.
Flies whine outside the trash can, wanting in
bad, like I would do or be you, or your twin,
beyond a shadow of my wildest doubts.
Flies whine outside the trash can, wanting in,
and the flies inside are dying to get out.

My Labor, and My Leisure Too

It's like looking at a Rothko every morning.
—Brian Bouldrey, regarding Lake Michigan

Two colors have never been two colors,
        or the horizon a line.
Lakeside parking sign poles were singing
        through empty screw holes,
a row of flutes some gargantuan Pan
        invisibly lipped and blew
on the terrace. I wandered, let the weather in,
        and opened for more as the force
of it played those unwitting pipes.
        The prairie grass reflected
what used to be a prairie town
        as sunlight set in the east—
the city tilted in the wrong direction,
        towards those wonky shapes
and stems of light like chicken fingers,
        chicken tenders dipped
in too much sweet, and what to do
        but eat. Pythagoras
had a golden thigh, some disciples said,
        and could be in two places at once;
there, with the dunes and roofs and bricks
        and brunettes of Michigan,
and here on the street I crossed diagonally,
        calling out his name.

One line never wrote the horizon.
        Moving along the edge
of the northeast wind, I could hear
        its volume inciting the lake
but did not feel it sounding past,
        a letter enveloped
and addressed to someone south of me.
        I read the cloud I walked
beside, its low drift translated
        on the turf. The height and speed
of an airplane touched me, its shadow
        the darting teasing slap
of a hand how quickly pulled away:
        native language of angels
who will not tell, and will not tell.
        What kind of grief was this?
A grief to keep, and keep forgetting.
        At a chapel, the bereaved in song:
"Amazing Grace," on bagpipes.
        I alternated verses with
"Because I Could Not Stop for Death."
        A line has never meant
there's something on the other side,
        another weather waiting.

I stood under colors, and counted,
        and divided by two.
I mostly forget what I do,
        and look for the life of the world

to come in the absent-minded afternoon.
      At one color I wondered
how many grapefruits he and I
      have shared, how many mornings.
Whenever I cut their globes I think
      "Equatorially"—
that's how he taught me to slice the whole
      into halves of isosceles
pockets to chew, a little juice
      on the cheeks. Half of me
is ocean, Tom Petty sings,
      half of me is sky.
The grapefruit light reframed the lake
      as dogs ran the grass above me,
again in grief. Two colors
      never made a horizon,
or the horizon a guarantee,
      not a single one.
At the end of the pier I forgot the pier,
      and the land, and the dusk, the day
I grew up very slowly and
      did not grow up at all.

Medea in Red River Gorge

As a sunbeam glimmers upon a room's walls, when water has just been poured from some cauldron into a pail, and here and there the dancing gleam quakes with the quick stream—just so, the girl's heart quivered in her breast.

—Apollonius, *Argonautica*, III: 756-760

Her hovel lets lost drivers know how lost they are,
cursing the crackling gravel road

                     and locking doors.

They always screech away and always her stomach jerks—
she knows so well the pull of gunning it in first.
But she goes to rhododendron groves

                              to forget,
a child beneath their titan leaves. Forgets again
on a chin of the ridge, studying the sandstone slabs

that study her:
                both tiger and lamb, both knife
and sacrifice. While life goes on, she suspects it does

not, and dreams of sailing on the world's first ship
which dolphin-women toss like a ball they will not drop
over wandering rocks and troubled waters. When she wakes,

14

how light
        she feels! but wonders could her biceps catch
and boost a keel, and would her breasts bounce like theirs,

exquisite bobbers upon waves, and if taken to suck
would they lactate sun
                or saltwater? She remembers

only edges, especially decks: standing starboard
watching shafts of sky fall and spread and lose
themselves in the sea, like immortality diffusing

through generations until it ends.
                        And him? He just sits
on the cat-scattered porch, whistles and whittles clean-

smelling white birch. The lines around his eyes are hers.
There are two ways of love, one that has not known hate,
and the other, and no mortal travels them together,

but Medea does.
        A girl can give up
                only so much blood.

Demiurge

At first you thought it meant a semi-desire,
a minor god of lesser drives, the tips of fingers
easily distracted from their intended shoulder,
a half-carafe of cabernet you almost ordered
for yourself at a sober table.
An undeniable impulse, rather cursorily
denied. A mistake you remember
when you think of other blunders
that call you their creator.

Mississippi Stasimon

With choruses of Euripidean slave women

Stepping on the banks my lovely ankles
splashed with mosquitoes and mud
and glare, so many lit candles
on the murk-loving water
that could have run
through the third-shift town
where I was born.
There's no nostalgia
a river can't bring and bear away.

> *Who then are these men*
> *who left the lovely water,*
> *green with reeds, of the Eurotas,*
> *or Dirce's holy streams,*
> *and made their way, made their way*
> *to this land wanting*
> *no one not its own,*
> *where the daughter of The God*
> *demands her altars and columned temples*
> *be stained with human blood?*

We go wading on the outskirts,
for every tragic city
must contain a river's curves,
a running commentary
worked out by God the scholar
who as a rule keeps tragedy
at a distance. He builds bridges
over detrital waters, dusty
dictionaries that list
his words on one side and ours
on the other, where we can see
the shallows in between.

Oh those thick-running streams
of tears streaking my cheeks
when, my city laid waste,
I was shipped away
by enemy oars and swords—
and through the trade
that swaps us for gold
I was brought to this
barbarian home

Alone on the shore
I'm alone with ghosts,
the worst kind of alone.
We can almost hear

the kudzu grow, the dew
evaporate, a wisp
of fog begin to exist.
Something starts to move
by the culvert, then gives up.
I cannot be alone enough.

Edged by water glossy blue
and fresh green helix leaves
I was drying crimson dresses
upon new shoots of reeds
in the golden gleams of sun
when I heard a noise to strike
my heart with pity, a cry no lyre
should ever imitate,
a woman's wail resisting something—
like a river nymph running away
in the mountains sings out a sorry strain
that echoes through rocky hollows
where Pan is forcing himself on her

Like the *keep still!,* the clenching teeth
when a bee lands on your skin,
a bustling force of drink or sting.
You wait and don't disturb him,
he smells nothing in you for him
but won't fly off. His hairy bee-knuckles

brush against the down
of the sweetest part of your forearm.
Bring your mouth near his
and exhale quick and hard.

If only I could travel
that lamp-lit chariot road
where the fine sunfire goes—
once I got above the chambers
of my home where I was a girl
then I'd stop the hurried flutter
of wings upon my back!

Animal families walk this hoof-and-paw path
my loneliness knows on its feet.
There are other solitaries here: a muskrat
floats, his belly to the sun his only
votive, offered and accepted at once.
Up north, station wagons
drive west across the river where it marks
the changing land. One child learns
she belongs to the mountains, another
confirms she's from the plains, and will return.

I think she may discover
the daughters of Leucippus by the river
or Athena's temple,
coming home as she will
at the time of dances

Let me know, ghosts, what kind
of song it is I'm singing
so I can be sure how it ends:
with a heroine's homecoming
or her undoing, with violence
or a guitar string plucked blue,
with a blessing, a deus ex
machina, or with a reunion
we thought as impossible
as rivers flowing uphill.

Cuticles

The shade decal stuck to the bus window exhausts
its glue at the break of noon, and flaps and peels
itself away into snow-hidden vineyards lost
in drifts of Michigan. When wintry cuticles
dry and thicken and fray, and not even a killer
icicle could cleanly pare the gamey skin,
I take to my father's old bad habit and tear
at the edges there. Chewable, some decisions,
like children's vitamins. Sunlight worries the raw
frozen lakes. He would grate his hands red with a grin
and spit anywhere, with relish, with a *puh-tah,*
with a certain daring
                              us to try and stop him.
The trees, their wild unrolling limbs all draped in white,
offer up fingers which they have no teeth to bite.

Myrmidons

Stepping off his ship, a young king
is recognized by the old
whose harbor and hills surround,
though the old king hasn't seen him
since the young king was a boy,
since the old king was young.

It can happen in these stories,
a demigodly prescience
or regal intuition
as to who, son of whom,
just entered the room, although
most faces' fame rode the world
through Rumor, that gardener
whose scattered seeds grow wild:

long tall tales of lustrous locks
tumbling down sculpted backs
or generous hefts of cleavage;
cheekbones to make any nymph weep
or suitor unsheathe his sword;
footfalls the dirt begs to feel.

Generic descriptions
prove ample and apt, as lovers
know as soon as they see each other,
as heroes pinpoint heroes

across battlefields, as a shield
depicts scenes whose details
are known by all who deal it blows.

Such powers of recognition
are displayed as often
as a wondrously complete lack:
a maiden shames the name of a goddess
who stands cloaked before her;
a woman's husband, gone for days
and in disguise, gains a private
audience in her chambers,

where she speaks of him to him
as gone; a divine mother advises
a half-mortal son, revealing
herself as she disappears,
and the human in him despairs,
grasps at the air that was her.

Some possess the gift to detect
that nothing is recognizable,
that some terrific change
has transfigured a place.
The young king, surveying
the island, asks the old,
Where are his boyhood friends?

The citizens who greeted him
are many and beautiful,
strong and dutiful, to be sure,
and gave him great pleasure to meet,
but the faces he expected? All
absent. The kingdom, different.

The old man tells of a ravaging
heaven-sent plague: the bodies
rotting through streets and forests
from a sickness so torturous
many hearts stopped still by their own
hands, rather than endure the horror.

As he was ready to end himself,
the old king saw ants, thousands
crawling on a sacred tree;
he prayed to the king of gods and
men that his people be restored
to the number of that colony.

Then, antennae sank into sockets;
hard shiny skin grew soft
and olive-smooth; the sex of each
creature manifested; hair streamed
out from rounded skulls; mandibles
shrank inward to mouths; two legs
were lost, two turned to arms,
and the last stood upright, shakily.

"Do you not see," said the old king
to the young, gesturing
beyond the palace, "something
of their former nature
in the way they move—divested
of instincts they still remember?

"But I've loved them, these child-like
denizens, since the moment
of alteranimation,
since they never doubted
their reason for being."
The old and the young man talk
of the young's upcoming war,
and before long, it is settled;
the Myrmidons will serve.

The Natural Look

Just look at the colors the shapely earth raises up . . .
—Propertius, *Elegies,* 1.2

So the poet persuaded his mistress to resist
makeup, myrrh, dresses—the glamour
of artifice. Do not think me cheaper,
he wrote, for lauding nakedness
and you, or using art to explain.
He arranged apples in her palms as she slept,
plaited her hair to his ideas.
My friend and I once hiked without a camera;
she rectangled her thumbs and fingers, clicked
her tongue across the shadow-stenciled hills.
On our faces we wore the wild civility
of the natural look—trying to look
like we don't try at all—in the trees
lovers initialed with car keys, by a sill
of slate inscribed, "Why do people write on rocks?"

Mimesis

I fear tragedy as we almost sleep,

around me his arms, or around him mine.

I fear the Fates for those who, busy being blissful,

are marked for tragedy. I couldn't say why.

I appeal to Aristotle—"Assume he and I are doomed.

You say tragic characters are of a higher value than comedic;

could this be a consolation?" Aristotle appears, in all earnestness.

He tells me he likes that picture of me and Plato at the Pergamon

in Berlin; the old man's solemn bust missing a nose,

his eyes wise and lifeless, as I am openmouthed smiling,

like a frolicsome nymph feeling her ass pinched, exclaiming, "Oh!"

Aristotle says to remember my face and listen to the Beach Boys.

"*Pet Sounds* is *aristos,* and 'Good Vibrations' is the embodiment,

yes," he said, "I said, embodiment of Friday night blossoming,

a first sight theme song, a saw playing itself in your head."

He would have included them in *Poetics,* these beach boys, as

none knew how to surf, and the only one who could swim, drowned.

"But first, my cow-eyed lady"—he loves those Homeric epithets—

"do listen to 'Don't Worry.'" Aristotle does not hit an attractive high note

as he pitches, *"Oh, what she does to me, when she makes love to me*

and she says, Don't worry, baby, everything will turn out alright."

My love turns over and I nuzzle my nose into his chest.

Oh his perfect armpit hair, how I adore it! He asks me

what my mumbles mean; am I laughing, or what?

Last Take

Before Holly Golightly quit the cab
to run in the rain, her hair was suddenly wet.
You wear your final fate like that,
like Holly Golightly, quitting the cab
to run to regain her rained-on Cat.
The backseat was dry as a fresh cigarette
when Holly Golightly quit the cab
to run in the rain, her hair already wet.

Crazy

As to when exactly Penelope knew
Odysseus was come home, people differ.
Did she decode her husband in the ragged beggar
and set the bow contest? Did she hear, contra Homer,
the ancient nurse gasp at his scar? What steadied her
to see his bet and bluff her bridal chamber?
I say it's after the slaughter and just before

he proves himself to be the one who built and knows
that bed: the moment they bicker, call each other
daimoniē. It is an odd apostrophe
you use if you're a baffled ancient Greek, baffled
by someone behaving so unreasonably
you cannot recognize them—a god, a daimon,
must be responsible. Between husband and wife,
a strange term of endearment, when endearment turns
estranged or strained. Alarm we could roughly translate:

Baby, don't be crazy. So far, he's convinced them all
but her. She keeps her distance once the blood's washed off
this man, anointed, looking good, and impatient.
Daimoniē! he says, and it's then she hears what
she cannot doubt—familiar lover's irritation.
His old *I can't believe you* voice makes her believe.
Daimoniē yourself, she says, and reels him in.

Veritas Caput

1.
Rivers ask you where
you're from and never
wait to hear the answer.

That faraway look
you get—now I know the place too,
now you'll see me there.

2.
If we spit off the Market Street Bridge
into the Mahoning
just to spit at something from above

part of us becomes Shenango, and Beaver and Ohio
all the way down to Cairo,
whose name it so much pleases me to say out loud

in how it marks the realm we live in, which does not please so much.
Then at Cairo Cairo that mouthful of us at Cairo
joins the earthquake river.

3.
Sources fascinate.
Fascination can pervert.
The Ojibwe name for the lake where the Mississippi rises

was changed by Henry Schoolcraft to sound Indian but be Latin
for men of letters: "Lake Itasca,"
the last four of *veritas,* the first two of *caput.*

Truth head. Truth mind. Truth headquarters. People say
Itasca means "true head" which is false.
That would be *verum caput,* or, if you want to be true

to Latin postpositive adjectives, *caput verum,*
which leaves us with either
Lake Erumca or Lake Aputve,

equally plausible to me unlearned as I am in this Schoolcrafted logic.
The former sounds hungry
and the latter satisfied:

not a hunger or satisfaction that is Indian
but Latin, salivating
tribute to men of Rome.

4.
Riverside in Youngstown we might have found
a fine little *locus amoenus*
were it not for the smell

of the Mahoning's funk.
No we cannot swim in and no
cannot drink the water where I'm from, cannot imagine

that. Here's my lap and a book,
drink up
the old pastorals.

5.
Its first name meant Elk Lake
which already spoke the truth, which already
was suggestive of a head, of antlers, nostrils, eyes.

Veritas caput. Say it
like an aging German and it sounds like something true
that's been broken: *veritas kaputt.*

6.
Where have you gone?
No river would ask.
Body of water,

another name for lover, rider, swimmer—
that head of yours is elsewhere
drinking from the source.

Two.

HOTELS, MOTELS, AND EXTENDED STAYS

The place where I prefer to live and work (and even rarer, where I wouldn't mind dying) is a hotel room . . .
— Albert Camus

The Ye Who Are Weary Come Home Motel

If you know the name, you've stayed the night.
Stepped right inside a room vacuumed
of the morning's strangers, who added to
its atmosphere. Have you and I
shared so much separately—a bed,
a book read there, a body ache?
Some rooms aren't rooms, most nights don't take
a night. Here, a lay to place your head.

The Buried in Sleep and Wine Hotel

Wake-up calls come as ghosts
whose death wounds, fresh along their flanks,
are little monsters, open enough to show
they are full of nothing inside.
These phantoms mean to announce
the city under attack, the insidious tricks
it fell for, how it even feasted its own demise
and rang with song and bedpost-banged walls
and now sleeps more deeply than its dead.
There is no pain like knowing the polis
is doomed. And so the shades
pontificate to terrify, convinced that terror
can't fail to get the dreamers on the move.
The great end of any dream is
the self-assurance none of it was real,
and the closing of eyes once again
to the hum of hallway ice machines,
distant and discrete from the burning walls.

The Things Will Never Be the Same Extended Stay Hotel

The desk has grown since yesterday, the cedar
hangers have alchemized to metal wire,
and the mirror is upside down, reflecting
a body-long wrinkle on the bed.
Redial button rings a stranger.
Even in the still life above the headboard,
rearrangement has transpired—yellow pears
knocked from the burnished bowl,
a corsage posed by the fiasco of Chianti,
and a chomped apple has been thrown in
so its tooth marks catch the light.
Someone has been here,
and the question is not identity
or intent, but how was it
for those bones to move in this room,
did a little toe bump the bed frame,
did that light switch turn on anything?
Pillows smell like the beloved's breath
after a beer, but among the suspects
the beloved does not number.

Route 3220: Chateau Bayou

Alone with two double beds
and a pullout sofa,

you set aside whatever you had
to do it with before you did

and called. I read you
and read to you some

studies in despair.
All must study, who would master.

The nature of a student is devotion
to her task.

N67: Stella Maris

You came to be undone,
historian of light,
by your histories.

To pile cuts of turf
and bricks of tea,
ignite the cottage stoves.

To walk the coastal road
whose edge refused
to be fulfilled by any will.

As if something worshipful
can be pronounced
by rituals of loneliness

that do not end in solitude.
Off-season guest
of a seaside town,

the boarded-up arcades
and beach gazebos peeling paint
made an initiate of you.

The Bump on a Log Hotel

The problem with waiting for the answer
is the answer
has been waiting longer.
That wish to be brave,
to rise before dawn and ride to the woods
and, as night burns into fog
hovering between dirt and treetops and
then gone, to wait for the answer—
that wish wakes late,
takes a to-go styrofoam coffee
to the closest municipal lot,
sinks in a slept-in yellow shirt upon clover
near accidental clumps of daffodils,
and understandably attracts bees.

The River of No Return Motel

Here you can sleep
with your favorite
song all night long.
You know how it
goes, how it knows
you. A Judy
with her Johnny
if ever there was.
The notes have bones
and plenty of
secrets to keep
with one who's true,
with only you.
Sha-la-la, ba
dum bop ba dee,
oh my wuh-oh-
oh-oh, wail-a-
ree, wail-a-ree.

The Let's Have a Cigarette and Assess the Situation Extended Stay Motel

In order to assess the situation,
a good wall is necessary
for strategic leaning
and contemplative exhalations
cast in smoke.
Across the state highway,
the strip mall sits for sale,
its parking lot lamps
empty umbrellas of spit and shine.
In this dead of the country
night, a passing trucker
shifts gears to meet a hill,
and the outline of his hat rim,
its rope trim as he drives by,
is too much detail,
liable to make him less
and so much more than
just anonymous.
Out of the distant turnpike din,
an exotic bird squawks
as though being mercilessly
mated or killed
in the stand of skinny trees
by the closed Kum & Go,
but it could be a trap,
a maniac with a recorder,

a brigand baiting the curious.
Neither twenty-four-hour drive-thru
will serve pedestrians.
Very few walls are no good
for leaning on.

I-80: Liberty Inn

Like a plucky Humpty Dumpty
you checked in with all your pills
to sit on the brink, great with your fall.

Or Odysseus, demanding
he be bound, then begging to be undone,
his bones let free to molder

in a heap beneath the bird-women.
He did not expect, so could not resist,
the promise of the Sirens' song:

not sex but knowledge,
intimate with the war,
what each man was to that war.

He did his lion roar and would have perished
just to hear the honey-throated harpies
tell him all about himself.

When bindings come loose,
the ropes that love pull tight.
Even a resentful crew will rescue

their king and captain, who shaped
sweet wax to plug their ears.
As if they could not hear what he heard.

We know the song, how
it puts on the hurt to meet the mouth
that sings. And we row.

A55: Brunch at the Grande Madame Bovarian

Eggs for the virgin and eggs for the crone
but never eggs between.
Serve with jam and cheese on toast
buttered with emphasis.

Our keyholes accommodate any eye,
our hallways are slippery slopes.
You packed your nose plugs? Take a dive
off cliffs, a digestive swim,

and mind you go no deeper than your waist,
or else the depths do call.
It's afternoon and I already taste,
you know, that evening feeling.

Catawba vines, Catawba vines!—
dangling dead down to the sea.
Lovers ought not redefine
what keeps each other breathing.

The Demolition Derby Motel

The last skipping stone of soap disappears
in its own suds, and water pipes gasp
their evacuation. Tire tracks traverse the walls—
what rides were given here, who took them, who
was taken? Derby-goers left early
this morning, coolers and cozies and high fives
in hand, headbutts in Mustang muscle shirts.
Across the potholes of the parking lot,
a foreman readies wrecking balls and yells
to any still inside to surrender ground.
And someone stands in a room stripped of itself,
envisioning what filled it to the brim—
two pairs of feet that talked under sheets
about stacks of pancakes and bacon that were
never gonna get made.

The Philoctetes Extended Stay Hotel

Throw a fat honey cake to the snakes
at registration if you want to see him,
your only chance of winning
the war: the man you marooned
nine years ago, the savior you left to suffer
a bite that oozed some wicked bile,
badly misinterpreted. What doesn't kill you
might kill you any day now,
you think as you knock. Perhaps he'd laugh
at that. The cave cracks opens just wide enough
for an outstretched hand to hang
a *NOLI ME TANGERE* sign on the doorknob.
Time, then, for a show of remorse. Or force.

The Ducks on a Whiskey River Motel

Who knows how deep they plunge
or long they dive, what crumbs they find,
how much is enough to resurface. Hard billed,
tough-as-rusty-nails willed, they kick
and keep kicking all the way down;
tails tucked, inborn buoyancy fought,
they swim until they're no longer ducks.

Route 6: Balmers Herberge

A field of forms
defined by lines
they make against
conclusive shades.

A pear picked up,
identified.
Knees fall on flattened
weeds while mountains
decide the stars.

And strangers talk
away their strangeness
with many kinds
of talk like touch.

Finish sentences
and nudge the napes
of necks as if
their shapeliness
had long been known.

Heaven happens,
extinguishes
the night before
its earthly end.

How could it last
in skin and fruit.
But don't be bitter.
Abandoned, do not
deny what you met.

The Only Living Girl in Chicago Extended Stay Hotel

Lord You Are My Solitude,
on the napkin left with an untaken tip.
Solitude never means just one, that
would be death. A walk is decided upon,
an exaggerated path woven again
around trunks. As night wades in, some
thing in the blood stirs to touch the bark.
Branches and leaves intone *Geronimo!*
altogether too calmly, as if it's nothing
to fall and touch the ground
for the first time. If a grandfather
were here he'd say *for the love of Pete
look at the time, turn on a light—
typing in the dark is bad on the eyes.*

The Drop-Kick Me Sweet Jesus
through the Goalposts of Life Motel

The blue-paned porthole opens to a field
someone else dreamed up, yellowed centuries ago.
It's pleasant to dream a stranger's sentimental dream,
and warm, like wearing a dead grandfather's sweater
and clenching the cuffs into fists. The walls are washed
as gray as that sweater, as if they wish to be
faring forth on the sea, away from all pastures.
The poorly appointed room has no door,
but one day, to some discerning outside eye,
the round window may look like a doorknob.

A841: The Corrie

We stayed in no one room or town
more than a night, and soon
would run ourselves right off the island,
escape the honeymoon.

In Blackwaterfoot, the hoary bed
and hallways smelled of horse.
And in our stained Lochranza suite,
a ghost wife paced the floor.

We drove the rental on and took
a room with a view of the sea
that never asked to be involved,
even panoramically.

The shower was a rubber hose
that did not fit the faucet.
The sheets wore hair of other women
who had stayed there and lost it.

Like plumes the curtains putrefied,
as if there dangled from the grout
peahens who aimed too high and hung
themselves while jumping out.

"Arise, my love, my fair one," you spake,
grabbing a flagon of Scotch,
and led me down the granite pier
to sit and drink and watch

the tide hard-flowing in the firth.
O my dove that art in the clefts
of the rock, I hardly slept in that bed
we had already left.

I-96: Amway Grand Plaza

We've been sleeping with shipwrecks
—if shipwrecks become sand
on Superior's shore, then
wash up on our feet in the tent—
and eating scraps of ash
whenever the breeze
peppered our meat
and mallow with embers.
Every hair is soaked
with smoke. Tonight,
in a week's first shower,
the smell of bonfire, bright
upon our heads and nethers,
will flare when doused with soap.

My body savors
such grubbiness, savors
getting clean once more,
and with yours. The accumulation
and the exfoliation, the nakedness
of a hotel before we're home.
We charge our phones,
luxuriate before we dress
and walk to dinner.
The world's still here, imagine!
I thought it might be gone.
Through the dusk I see a heron
standing in the river.
And you see silver horses, risen.

The I'm Not as Good as I Once Was, but I'm as Good Once as I Ever Was Motel

The sailboat filled with soil
is set on the lawn by the great lake,
is listing slightly starboard
from such anchorage. Nothing sprouts
from its survey of black dirt;
but the distressed blue wooden beams of its hull,
and the rusted blue iron handrails
along the gravel path, and the insular blue
of the great lake sky all seem destined
to coalesce and grow old together here today.
Everything good is better in syntax,
next to something else.
A couple at the end of the middle of their lives
sit close on a bench, taking in
these moving gardens of juxtaposition.
On the beach a man makes his long-tailed kite
waltz in serpentine curves coloring space.
The couple stands to walk through a field
where the great lakeshore collation of tall grass and oaks
has been fenced off and designated
an IBA (Important Bird Area),
and through that area they agree
arm in arm, and around them
important wings fly and settle and fly, and again.

SR 165: Western Reserve

At a crossroads where the frontier once stopped
stands a falling down house, a family
history, happy to have you for the night.
Please disregard the mess, their floors that creak
like prophets of rottenness, the piles
of scat shaped like ammunition
for Cousin's BB gun, the half-collapsed
columns of ceiling beams, like so many
elbows a chin leans on. Be not afraid
of the shambles, for all of your travels
in this country will lead you to shambles,
but some are spruced up. Mostly the ghosts will
make no fuss—the Great Depression chickens
Great-grandmother kept in the yard and let
in the kitchen, the hired hands retired with
their scythes to the barn, the men who spent hours
in blackberry thickets and the women
whose flour, sugar, and butter waited for
those buckets to fill. Oh hello, Sister,
Grandma greets her only daughter. You can
hear her tonight, weeping why pioneers
ever left, while you wonder when you'll leave.
The illusion of your rented room, the same
as some illusions of the land—that what
you pay for is yours—secures you to sleep.

The Grant Me the Stamina to Pray
Extended Stay Motel

To quiet the mind into nothingness
is not the task. To keep the mind quiet
on a single thing, or perhaps a string
of single things, to think not of the thought
but just to think, intimate with the unknown—
what maintenance of the heart
that takes, what unaccustomedly narrow
points must stay pinned. As if a meteor sails
through the awful silence of outer space, but then
the daily offering must be drawn from the purse
always, always the elbows or knees
get sore. The eyestrings
must be held taut with that which has no eyes,
which grants the wherewithal to ask
before it tenders any yield.

The Western Edge of a Time Zone Hotel

Not far from here a meadow marks the line
of the longest sun and brightest time human
arrangement of such things allows—
a map to the meadow informs every bedside drawer.
Its eagles dart close as prairie moths,
grasshoppers fly ahead of footsteps
with the hum and herald of rotary phones,
and trees wave in the light like crowds at concerts
who wanted the lawn tickets they got
for the amphitheater show, would not wish
for anything else. A beautiful place
to die, the underworld rising up
through golden grains and purple-tipped spears
and weeds that sprout their own billowy cosmos
for heads and blood-red sumac buds sculpted
by wind—to see the grim one coming through all that,
to claim not a wife but the love or despair
of one life. To be there
to be told however it went down it's done,
in the meadow with its manifold vantages of hours
over there, where they've already happened,
and that way, where they are still, or about to be.

Three.

I, AUGUSTINE I–XIII

. . . so that I might "apprehend him
in whom I am also
apprehended" . .
    — Augustine, *Confessions,* Book XI, 39

Si Quaeris

If you seek a pleasant peninsula, just look around
—State motto of Michigan

The air you breathe freezes
on your beard, icicled
strands like gleaming stands of trees.
I bring my mouth, a scald
to still air, to your chin
and with my wordless tongue
I eat your breath. The only hints
the ground lets slip into the open
of how hot the earth gets in her middle
are the geysers, the springs, the steam risen
to shape the very air it veils.
I take your gloved hand in my gloved hand
again, that you might part your mouth
and say—something you have not been taught.

Augustine I

Praising you, I begin, but how
did I begin to praise?
Deus meus, dear muse my God,
give me to know how men,

the fractured fraction of all creation
we are, first learn to talk
to you—does need of you precede
our knowing you, or must

we know to need? To call then praise,
or does praise shape the call?
But how to call without belief,
or believe before the ache

of soul and marrow's reach for you?
O Lord, settle me down—
who seeks will find, who finds will praise,
who needs will know what is

needful. If sky and earth and we
can bear your signature,
why yearn for what composes us?
Why so much desire when

entirety surrounds entirely?
As if I'd like to find
one corner where you were not,
so I could call, "Here!"

and as you spilled into that square
of concrete, finally
I could feel filled. Folly, Lord, yes,
and yet—I confess this voice

you lend me calls you within me,
and skies and earth and skies,
inflated full but not defined.
Is origin our end?

Easter

Mid-morning, a girl and dog attend the woods,
the lilies of the valley just shy thin shoots.
The Boy Scouts' flying squirrel huts are crooked
after last night's storm, and the woody vines tangled loops,

depending. Girl palms the oak she calls half hers,
two trunks from one. Dog pees on a painted stone.
Off trail and leash, paw prints of mud daub girl's jeans:
little wolf, she calls the dog. Little lamb, goat,

little kangaroo, little bat, sea lion,
little goose, cow, muskrat, water buffalo,
little antelope, dolphin, Rodent of Unusual Size,
little griffin, cupbearer, acolyte of logs.

Dog nibbles on new grass, lifts nostrils to air.
Girl stares up at branches refracting the sun:
her expectation of a vision, her lack
of surprise should one come. Going home she must

pick up milk at the town's only open store.
Dog sits in the car with the radio on.
Under the fluorescence, products appear lush
and skin pale. Pastel candy's in the sale bins,

basket toys are marked down: fuzzy ducklings
diapered in cracked halves of eggshells, girl bunnies
and boy robins in smart petticoats and suits.
Some can talk, and wear stickers—Squeeze Me, Try Me.

Augustine II

There was a tree, as there often is,
and the reins on us boys were loose.
A tree between grapevines and pigpens,
a tree so blessedly fat with pears,
lackluster fruit we never wanted—
that tree got under our skin, Lord,
dangling low the way it did, laden.
One tempestuous night, we schemed
the heist, scornful of any purpose
but to leave its limbs denuded.

We plucked and ran with overloaded
armfuls, took for the taking thrill.
Why do you let it feel so good, God,
to break the laws you forge in us?
We could not eat all that dirty-sweet
flesh, and threw the rest to the pigs.

Snoring, some grunted as pears thudded
their snouts and rumps. A bruised bad fruit
lands with a foul splash in dungy mud:
such was my soul, behold, wicked
and smitten with wickedness itself!
Whence can it come, this sweet rapture
in wrong, wrong acts, the relish thus wrought,
lines beloved to walk and cross
because they run crooked? I know not.
Whose pear tree, I can't remember.

★ ★ ★

Breviarium

In amateur romantic languor
I moved all over town, waiting
for the world to part its mouth and draw
close to mine. It is of a piece
with me, to presume what I want wants
me back, and pieces fall together
like strangers shocked at the familiar

feel of one another. But you,
oh my most unsurprisable
Lord, lift not a brow. Some have chased you
like a desire, like a beloved
in whom they see their own reflection,
you who must be loved like nothing

else. To these you say, So you wish to
know yourself? Fog up every mirror
with all your hot air, and run along
where the murkier surfaces
play. The past becomes a pool that waits
to show your face. Or a desert.

Bonfire

"I love rabbits," you're supposed to say
around a bonfire when wind blows smoke
in your face. Admit it—you love rabbits—
and the air, previously unaware
of your existence, relents and lets rise
the kind sting, absorbing, acidic
to the slightly alkaline glaze of your eyes.
The wind that retreats will return
and things could get crazy: that's when
you repeat it, over and over until
the great breath defers to this
old trick. A good fire, we say,
and skies start to rain water's quiet.
It blossoms hazy, the smoke hit with what
should feel like grace, and the wood
yelps a little, burns all the more
when heaven's heel tries to put it out.
Come back and go away again.
I love rabbits, I love rabbits, I love rabbits.

Augustine III

Upon the sweltering stage of Carthage
I walked hot coal floorboards and yearned
from depths of my soul never known until
aflame. I loved to love, to love removed
from love, I loved to contemplate myself
as lover, loved the melting motion of
new bodies newly known, loved mine as one
of them, loved love stories that revealed me
protagonizing each object desired.
And when lovers shouted my name across
steamy crowds, oh, the gleaming embers stirred.
How sweet the bile, how sensual the chains!

A strange starvation, that of you, my God:
the worse nourished, all the less I hungered.
Theatergoers, we were the theater—
the sighs I heaved from my seat, enraptured,
were no far cry from those in lovers' arms,
false love as cathartic as tragedies.

The Carthaginian I've still in me
exquisitely thrills, weeps to tell these tales.
I keep a snuffer close by his candle
that would flare to cast a glow as we fall
all over each other, and over again.

Cleavage

My upside-down vista skirted by shade,
on my back headfirst on a downhill grade,
I want you to stay, though it's me who moves,
lying high below the Ohio River
drenched with you. Here is skin that's been all winter
covered, here is gravity, there its shove
away from clothes, zephyrphilic linens
to disclose hips and delighted armpits
to your corona. Bumblebees tango-dip
themselves on necks of clover, wrens enliven
the hedges they hide in, and an ant takes
his stand on my hand as we spin into night.
As if my universe revolves around the likes
of you! Whom some longitude line overtakes,
and the cool comes on. My ex used to say,
after the breakup and before we stopped
messing around, "I hate to see you go, but
I love to watch you walk away."

Augustine IV

You knew I loved him, and you knew
I did not know how to love
beyond possession, no doubt because
he let himself be mine. But when the fever drew
his final breath to you, all things became his lack:
the signposts that once called out, "Here he comes!,"
on the paths of thoughts we took together, to summits
of passions in that less-than-year. And at my back
I could always hear your advance, fountain
of mercy, God of vengeance. On his deathbed
he renounced me, doubly left me where I had
to leave. Nothing humbles like a hometown.
Half my soul, I called him, halfway to you.
He died believing, in a fever I'd live through.

★ ★ ★

Breviarium

I barked against you like a stupid hound
chained to a stake he cannot see is free
from the ground. I wrote a lost book, *On Beauty
and Decorum,* bedecked my head with garlands
from poetry contests, invested my credit
in astrologer hoaxes, made speeches, got
Aristotle. Why should I tell, my God,
my foolish life to you who authored it?
It's like sitting on a mountaintop rock
and telling the hills across the valley
how clearly you can trace the path you walked
over them. It's like being so startled to see,
upon return from holiday, your home unchanged
that you say, You still are here! You're still the same.

Highway 101

A stone arch is pinned by a neon blue cross, thin
as veins in my rearview. The shapes of cows in coastal pastures
make this, the far end of twilight, seem further,
and if we were at home my mother might say *pull over,*
let's see them. But we are somewhere we've never been,
I drive us through snowy canyons of mountains
whose names we don't know, we only say oh, my God, and then

they become the sky. She flinches at the fog, tries to divine
ahead of the headlights. I sing, *I can't go to Paradise*
no more, I killed a man back there. She looks astray,
gives a faint sway of the shoulders. A blue and red OPEN sign
some shopkeeper forgot to turn off blinks and backs away,
and out loud I count down the white miles to Coos Bay.
On a scale of Hail Mary's she has rated these drives,
in the unsettled accounts of her hands. Tonight is a nine.

Augustine V

Outweeping ocean waves, my mother beat
her chest at Carthage, begrudging water
its route to Rome, where she'd accompany me
(Yes? she asked) if I would not stay. Her groans,
as she held me who would deceive her, whipped

my heart as I resolved to leave her, whipped
by grief of too great desire, carnal groan
of mothers to hold the boat their waters
of womb set sail. At the shrine of *beatus*
Cyprian she spent the night without me

and begged the saint to stay me, to keep me
near her always. I sailed off, my heartbeat
unknown to the ocean's, the ship a whip-
crack cresting dawn, and land shrank as water
and wind enfolded. And she woke to groan

and curse her trickster son, gone in the roan-
skinned sea of morning, seeking with groans me
who was begot with groans, Eve's ancient beat.
She said a prayer, went home. The journey whipped
me into a fever no Roman water

could calm; wading in Stygian waters
whose waves would rise like hands to slap my hips,
I dreamt of blood-red beds and moons and groans
of human houses falling down around me,
refusing baptism, a living deadbeat.

Across the whipped and beaten sea, she prayed
for me, whom she groaned so long to deliver
to the spirit on the water.

★ ★ ★

Breviarium

Accept these admissions, this crafting hand
of this tongue that has tasted; these bones, from the feet's
intricacies to spinal line, conquer
to heal, my Dominus, brush the dust of roads
that burned my eyes and stained those days of years.

There are none who hide their face from yours, ears
covered like children singing la-la road
songs to forget the road, their ostrich feet
upon the ground they bury heads and hands
in. You are there, you witness all and conquer

unknowing hearts to knowledge, unconquered
wills becalmed. We fill our days, busy our hands
as even animals animate years,
measure by mortal definition feet
of distance, travel believing all roads

lead to other roads, and wander these hard roads
until we wonder. Once wanting, we're conquered
by you, our founder, who find us to hand
us back our lives. One day of any year,
you appear at the breakfast table, your feet

on a chair—your unmoved mover's feet
the floorboards creaked beneath for years
from a secret room, wallpapered off in broad
patterns of stripes and bouquets like a recurring
dream. We tear it off, in strips, with our hands.

Such were the roads and works of hands in my
twenty-ninth year; I was less defeated
and closer to my conqueror.

Who Art in Heaven

That first verb of the Pater Noster
and he was a painter, a painter who sat
on a small backless stool,

as white cords of hair covered
the knot of his smock strings,
and he bent over oils and brushed slow strokes

onto a canvas that I,
although I'd imagined the scene,
could not see clearly.

He was being painted, too—
with many words we made
as if to fix him, to fit a frame around an abstract shape,

or magnify a crisp landscape, defined
by its infinity. And he was paint,
the berries and the blood and the watercolor shadows

cast on those kneeling close
underneath the stained-glass stories.
He was the material we and he used

to approach each other.
Painter, painting, paint—
my first idea of a trinity.

Augustine VI

My barefaced panegyrics for the beardless boy emperor
were goading me—frenetic I paced Milan, past a beggar
drunk at noon, guffawing, feet propped on the gutter,
his face at ease, with dimpled smile.

Those eyes, outlined by wear of living hard, glittered merry,
and dirt-rimmed fingernails waved skyward telling stories
punctuated with clicks of coins, to buy more cheap cherry
wine to swill, and a little to spill.

To honors, money, marriage, I aspired and you chuckled,
Lord, at the grip ambition, anxiety, and opinion held
on me, and you presented him whose face spelled, if misspelled,
a happiness I could not achieve.

I sought pride and success through lies, and his pleasure arrived
through well-wishes of passersby; bombastic-lipped I lived
mendacious constant struggles, charitably he survived;
all my comfort was killing me.

He was having a good old time, worthless bum though he was,
and I, just as worthless, more miserable, without a buzz
to gladden head and freshen step, pretended higher cause
for my imperial pantomime.

What glory lies outside you, who rebreak our broken bones
to heal correctly? Equally inglorious that day, the both
of us, but joyful he pretended nothing, and would doze
off his poison. I'd wake with mine.

★ ★ ★

Breviarium

There are days on earth we're struck, Lord, by the thought we haven't done
a thing, and we're nearing thirty, and first felt the blazing sun,
the fever to create, fifteen years ago . . . Has it been that long?
Can you know that, what you can't feel?

When my mother's visions of my marriage smelled strange to her tongue,
she called it off—her weakness, not your wish. My one love long gone,
I took an interim mistress, my dark delights kept on.
Can you not know what you can't know?

Tribute

Ocean-educated, the boulders demur
to bide time with me spending mine on their contours,
composites of dense breath whose density
might pulse. I pass a crab moving slowly,
careless who sees he's dying, into a washed

up lobster pot: airy containment he chose
for himself. He eyes me, lifts a pincer,
and empties out. A trawler slow-motors
through floating fields of buoys, its stereo
blasting "Hurts So Good." Guitar riffs echo

through shoreline rocks, marked with the run of the tide's
attentive tongue, or tapered into profiles,
faces of whales and sharks. "Sometimes love don't
feel like it should," I serenade the stone beasts.
A rib cage decays on the pebble beach

with a single leg and hoof still attached.
I put my hand between the bones, extract
a green beer bottle, its white horse's head.
From the glass-lined tanks of Old Latrobe
it comes from the mountain springs to you,

as a tribute to your good taste. The boat
leaves all the island circumscribed by bait
and quiet. Distant sunning seals bark away.
Back in my landlocked home, old Marvin Oates
used to walk out the door winking, *I'm gonna go*

check my traps. He would state his full name as
Marvin Guy Abraham Lincoln Hungry Oates.
When he was green and young, so was the earth,
and it gave him fresh catches, hung on a thread
of allure, the same that sews the quick to the dead.

Augustine VII

Reading, I had a vision and you
were the closest you'd ever been,
yourself the door you opened wide.
I entered and saw by the eye
of my soul, above my soul's eye,
ineluctable light.

Not the light of streets and forests,
of bodies' or planets' glow,
nor some grander version of sun
so multiplied it blinds
or swallows. A light apart, not above
my mind, as oil surfaces

water, or skies impose the shores
that bound them. A light better
than me below, than me it made,
its heir, its earth, its son.
It knew something true to announce
by shining, some eternity.

Love knows this light, its residence
where these abstractions get
mixed up, confusion's holy house.
Let me be that confused
with you my God, you I want to breathe
all day and all of the night,

your truth where I am not yet lit.
You called, "I am who is,"
from far away, from where we wait
to be translated with all
your words. If words are thoughts. And if
they are not, then wordlessly.

The Angelization of Mr. Vodka

Yes so Siobhán McKenna was reading Molly Bloom like a song-throated bird of prey all of us at the seminar table the smooth sure wood and splintered nicks of it were on the mattress with her in the hillside heather with her until John lifted the diamond's loose needle from the vinyl grooves a light lily touch that takes to leave the air unscratched but he did not turn off the player so during Anya's presentation on radio and its well epistemopoetical effects on Joyce [voices elbowing enveloping voices wild mutts of language at each other's necks in play death grips manic maenad frequencies] just as she spoke the words "man-made static" those air waves in the record player began to hum teeming with human din and I was sure it was him alone in Toledo once I was reading such dread Vesuvian sensations I get reading sometimes visions unseen but felt Nietzsches or sainted half-mad thinkers staggering to come right through my pages spread for it in the fast grassy heat of the read but so in Toledo alone the Penelope chapter in my lap on Amelia's balcony a voice called "Baby get over HERE" a sonofabitch voice in a foul needful mood "Ain't MESSing around got something for ya" and I wondered has the god come to me does a colossal swan with a colossal hard-on wait anon in the alcove I followed his voice to the powered stereo he streamed out through the big block speakers and I turned him off just as Amelia materialized a voice? she said oh that was Mr. Vodka and explained he conducts all his Old West End business in a van with ten-foot antennas and two-way radios he gets into everyone's homes saying such things yes he's been asked to stop no that's not his real name her dad has just always called him Mr. Vodka freed from flesh an angel of electricity his center as everywhere and his borders as limitless as Augustine's God being in the air makes an angel of you too Mr. Joyce the woman's voice I read above yours the dirty demands I heard under Jove Mr. Vodka who loves his label as himself and you who loved all things that flow and what flows like radio the turn of a dial the push of yes a big power button but now turn off the lonely channels can't leave them open all the time Mrs. Bloom says yes because a woman whatever she does she knows where to stop sure Siobhán McKenna read that like a clawed bird

Augustine VIII

As there is no pleasure in food and drink
unless hunger and thirst prevail—
see the drunk eat salt and lovers refrain,
the earthly tongue by the bit lip
denied, delayed to please all the more—
just so, my errant trail to you,
as I moaned and snoozed and caught my yawns
in the bodied heat of sheets.
How long had I asked how much longer
before I gave my whole lusty
soul to you? I was done with myself
and fled to the garden, my want
translated by its bed of impatiens
that burst so easily to the touch.

Talking to myself in psalms, the tongue
to speak to you, feverish now
for your measureless cool, my Lord,
upon the brink of sanity
I seemed somewhat mad, monstrous-eyed.
Alypius, a man with whom
a man who needs company can be
alone, sat as I ran to fall
at the roots of a tree and wept at my past,
the hands and locks it laid on me,
the grand procrastinator prostrate
beneath boughs of figs and fig leaves.

And then I heard the chants of children,
with no children in sight—"Pick up
and read, pick up and read"—eerie song!
and with an ancient love of signs
I opened at Paul addressing the Romans
and read what I needed to. Not much
can be said of the peace I gained then,
its nakedness. We told my mother;
she blessed my faith as far better
than grandchildren, and those things she thought
she wanted begotten of me.

★ ★ ★

Breviarium

I so feared you would answer my prayers,
you who transmute our grief to joy—

Dear God, part of me did love my grief.
I begged, "Make me chaste, O Maker,

but not yet, not yet." How must we look,
immutable one, your unfixed

and mixed up crazy creatures for whom
the deeper the abyss, so much

the sweeter. We've inherited that
from you, the parent who adores

the prodigal child's broken return,
the long-shouldered parcel of sins

well-traveled, more than the constancy
of the world-poor one who remained—

Love me then. Love all these aches that map
the way of crawling back to you.

Wings on Wheels

This morning the ivy on the wall predicts
a grand realignment in spatial time
— for today I fly for to see my love,
I dress and press my lips —

                              Granville dead-ends
into the lake, where wishy-washy clouds
shift shape to let spill one shaft of such light
any pilgrim's heart would disrobe to swim out to
— for today I fly for to see my love,
my travel apple packed —

                              A tricky carrot
like any god, that sun, who at the drop of a hat
appears everywhere, blasting even the can
of High Life balanced on a white banister
— for today I fly for to see my love,
"Come and Get Me!" says a 7-Eleven
banner for a Slurpee —

                              In terminal H
a buzz-cut kid tosses a Nerf to the zenith
of the birdshit-and-insect-spattered skylight
— for today I fly for to see my love,
and the boy will fly with his football —

                              An old man
in plaid reminds me of Ireland, like the alleyway

off Lakewood behind the church
where the scratched white brick back wall
and the ashy brick chimney stack
and the white sliding slants
of steeple remind me of Ireland
or some feeling called Ireland, a feeling
that I can call what I want what I want
— for today I fly for to see my love
to tell him it's half-true, that absence makes the heart —

Augustine IX

In Ostia we overlooked
a garden, my mother
and I, not long before her death,
and glimpsed eternity,
our foreheads dewy with you who reign,
and with the mouths of our hearts

we panted, contemplated far
beyond the earth, even
its headiest delights which pale
and wane next to you, and rose
beyond the sun and moon and even
heaven's trackless trains,

we climbed our minds and overtook
them too, and stood in soft green
smoldering, for to have been or be
about to be, that plain
does not involve these tenses,
but only is, and is

the joy of God and only yours
to know, and ours to drop
down to our knees and watch it go,
the vision gone as soon
as we saw we could not exist with it,
but all we could do we did,

leaving an emblem of ourselves there,
anonymous as a stone,
and sighing after it we returned
where words begin and end.
And all while we talked, we two alone,
below us the Tiber flowed.

★ ★ ★

Breviarium

By baptismal pools my mother lives
and takes fine sips of holy wine
from unattended tabernacles.

She knows the words to all the hymns,
removes the dedicated candles
burned down to beeswax stubs of prayer.

Your lady of the altars, Lord,
my hope, my sparrow, has herself
become the altar, the incense smoke

and censer, every rosary.
Your handmaid transubstantiated
into the paint of all your saints,

the bowl of consecrated water
and the cool clean salve, clear within.
I see my face reflected daily

there in hers, at the church's doors.
I dip my fingers and in your name
she makes the sign of the cross on me.

On the Heat of Upstate Travel in the Advancing Polar Air

Winterreise Winterreise
he was saying as I woke him
first a blanket then a ride
a winter journey
he'd been dreaming in *vinter*

> *vinter   vinter*
> Driver take the Amstutz
> to the shores of the Dead River
> we have packed our sandwiches

> > of tavern ham and fig jam
> > winter wants him and I am
> > *vintering*
> > tavern ham fig jam
> > aged and crumbling cheese
> > on old world rye to be had
> > on a headland of sand
> > the sign says
> > could wash out any minute

> what grain what grape what vintage
> are we drinking
> this is one of those days we disappear for years

the Orthodox
don't like all the torment of Western churches
our demons' gleeful torturing
in Renaissance splay across canvas and domes
the dimpled asses of *putti* smiling on
concerned but unable to help
and fairly certain none of that will happen
to them

    No the long beards and veils of the East believe
    God's love is fire
    and the virtuous experience it as bliss
    and all others as a burning
    a cleansing a purgation
    that gets rid
    of anything but bliss
    for anyone

        drinking a winter journey
        he's still dreaming
        of ways to worship despite himself to get beside that fire

    I've never had Swiss like this
    old world old
    dry hard world
    all these ingredients
    what a pleasure to chew
    on the beautiful shores
    at the Dead River's mouth

bit by bit a cold sandwich hits
our hot stomachs

until we're filled we need we await disasters
like this weather
don't call it a polar vortex
meteorologists say
it's just winter
vinter   vinter

Driver take the Amstutz
past the factory on the lake
its bricks are singing
some red rye blues
some mortar ballads of hard-pressed fruit
a song of vines and times so cold it killed bricks
against the blanket waters
against a ride of aged blue

factory on the lake
dark intestines
flame within
I have felt the bliss
and the burning too

Augustine X

May I know you as I am known by you,
stripped bare. You are so loved and so desired
I blush and kick myself and can't be pleased
unless pleasure comes from you, heartbreaker.
Your fingertip how slightly brushes down

the navel of naked still lakes, and logs
and grasses tremble at the treble, touched
that they exist. I have a part in that wood
and water, remembering how I forget
how you are always going on around me:

the grainy glow backlit behind a crowd
and meadow grass on fire with ferocious gold
and slides of light through vintage windowpanes
or pale-webbed pines that show dust motes and moths
as clashing planets, the sky that falls each day

into an ordinary oblivion.
There is no end to what I can forget.
And memory demands we find ourselves
mysterious. How do you dwell in me,
my Dominus, my domicile? As a feeling

I left home without something important?
As my inscrutable handwritten notes?
As a smell that makes me dizzy for myself,
my past, enigma I can almost name?
No penitent more passionate than when

I remember how late I loved you:
so very late in loving you, beauty
older than the world and never more here
than now, so late! You were within and I
was without, an ingrate in a world of grace.

You called, and your voice annihilated night,
you gleamed and lit up all my silences,
I tasted and now I pant for your touch,
your scent, I inhale it all over again
so my lips remember that first full cup.

You let me forget the chasm between us
embedded in me, you let me enter
a sweetness which if perfected would mean
another existence. Do I recall
myself because the strange mood must end?
Such moods cannot bear the memory of what I am.

Ayr

Christmas shops open all year.
How to bear the long-lit hours
Perfecting the slow kill of summer?
Like a lion the sun stalks the clock tower.
Sometimes I think about Ayr.

Cobblestones are dry with beer
And spit, and spotted with chips,
The pre- and mid-digestion bits.
Heartbeats get clogged from so many fried giblets.
Sometimes I think about Ayr.

And Ayrshire, too—slack-jawed glares
Of the Black Bull's proprietress,
Her right pinky pulling down her lip.
The filmy aquarium veils depressed fish.
Sometimes I think about Ayr.

The Maybole train station wears
Advertisements for cheap cheese
And cigarettes by the old bowling green,
Where junkies stash packages in shrubberies.
Sometimes I think about Ayr.

And Robert the bard—oh, bard!
You're a museum, marketed
In ad campaigns of italic words.
Your walks are paved, your thatched cottage replicated.
Sometimes I think about Ayr.

We left on the next ferry
Out of Stranraer when we tired
Of being asked, "Why are you here?"
Even the River Ayr leaves Ayr
For everywhere.

From the poop I saw a pair
Of cows who climbed the shire's stairs
Of pasture hills to stand and stare, their posture
magnificently bare of poise and purpose.
Were they happy there?

Augustine XI

Yours are the days and the night too is yours,
my Lord, and dense eternal books of earth
and heaven's heaven. My prayers remain yours,
you who know my need, and those deer are yours,
in scripture's obscure woods, the roes who long
to prove curative these hard words of yours—
we watch them ruminate on your laws, yours
the gold flanks glimmering through leaves of time.
I unravel your Word and look for time
in the twine; that is most perfectly yours
and may only be mine if mortal tongues
interpret the pearls you refine on tongues.

Grant what I love, for love. Grant that my tongue
may speak your tongue as it longs to be yours.
In the beginning you made, so your tongue
told Moses, heaven and earth, fiery tongues
of cloud and stone. Moses wrote and left earth
but if I'd heard your story from his tongue
I would know its truth, no matter his tongue—
Hebrew, Greek, barbarian—or how long
or little he spoke words of men who long.
In the little house of my head the tongue
of your son tells me what's true over time,
and at the last he'll tell the truth of time.

You anticipate all times, but not in time.
Creator, words could not fall from your tongue
to spark our world of matter on which time
here depends, where material words need time
to pass, eternal draughtsman, to be yours
and ours. In the beginning of our time
you made heaven and earth, heaven which time
cannot touch, and the slugs and steeds of earth's
mutability. You made! heaven and earth.
It strikes my heart without hurt every time,
fearing what I'm so far from as I long
for and love its nearness, which I've loved long.

To be he who knows what is time! As long
as no one asks, I know. There was no time
when there was no time. What minute is long,
what year? A sound still sounding can't be long,
can't be measured till it ends on our tongue.
Time wants surprises and can wait a long
time. My shepherd, let me call nothing long
except distance from our pastures to yours,
how long our bleats carry over greens of yours.
As I speak my heart beats and I speak long
and splash in tides and timetables of earth,
await the moon's wane, her mouth full of earth.

The mouth expects the past labors of earth
to resurface in rhythms we mark long
or short and fall into future songs of earth.

To recite a psalm is to remake earth,
refashioning the whole by one part in time.
The sun will rise, I say, and then the earth
outdoes me, tilts her chin and dawning tongue.
My heart's a lantern as real as my tongue
in my mouth as I serve and alter earth,
as changed I change in my time, unlike yours
where unchanged you change, make all you've made yours.

I could know time if you said, "This is yours,"
as you gave me to know a psalm, my tongue
its vessel reinvented, and then time
would sing me. But time dissolves those who long
to intimate you in their time on earth.

Onion

The shanks are braising
and the west sets,
sunning the window flushed
with a little stovetop sweat,
the palest red residue
of flame's exhalations,
of the kiln in the clouds,
of the lamb's blood on hands
I bring to my chest.
The lurid star
I stare at, too straight ahead,
averts my gaze
to how it renames
the remains behind me,

how mercy works.
It lights up the vine
tomatoes' insides
through a blue glass bowl
and fills with glints
the wedding crystal
goblets in the pantry,
wanting wine with dinner.
I hum, return to knife
and cutting board.
The Lord knows the tender
love songs I sing to him,
but you, my emerald-
eyed onion, never.

Augustine XII

And let me recreate again
   creation. Earth at first was invisible
    and uncomposed, a shadow
     above the abyss. And we
      can imagine none of it,
    we who think in shapes and call
   you Father. A huge sea sponge
saturated by endless sea—
   that's how I used to think
    of earthly life, drenched in but apart from
     your infinity. In the beginning
    you made everything
   change. Even my vows, mutable
in these dreams I cannot check,
where I love and love
   to love again, in the unmade bed
    of my head. And wake to hate
     my waif of a soul.
     I saw a strand of my own gray hair
    caught in a stray spider's web,
  and despaired to die, and
despaired once more
   that I would shrink from being
    like the earth at first,
     invisible and uncomposed.
     I could quarrel over every word
    of yours, Lord, as do men

who think their arguments serve you:
you, a mosaic of meanings,
    of differing truths that do not undo
        each other. As when people gather
            along spans of water
                to watch suns or moons rise or set,
            and to each one's gaze
    the long reflecting ripples glitter
straight to their own feet;
    just so, you show yourself.
        If those single visions
            overlapped, what blaze!
            Let him who glimpses it
        make confession to you.
    Let him who does not
confess this, too.

Midnight Mass

At what no one saw in the woods, dogs barked.
The moon once swaddled sky, hanging as huge
as a face above one's bed—her sleepy fugue
has publicized earth's weakened pull. We parked
above a river today, drank a few beers
on a rose and cream granite bar. You prince.
We slept through the solstice lunar eclipse,
but I've seen bare clear suns redden your hair.
Wonder counselor, the prophet called the babe.
Babe, you call me, you who called all the girls
you knew women. We sang "Joy to the World,"
my arm in yours. How the world has aged!
It saddened you once, but be saddened no more.
Whatever stirred the dogs approaches the door.

Augustine XIII

My Lord of mercy, radiate
your light on me, my words
of which you have no need, a gate
to your unfenced pastures.

Open the firmament, its creed,
your book in cloudy form,
which angels teach us how to read
by matchsticks' astral scores.

Let there be light, you said, and light
of no sentence became—
who heard the crack, saw tongues of night
split with the branding flame?

Run everywhere, you holy fires,
you beauties, keep me warm,
your arms to hug my life, a bird
alive with living worm.

The apple bitten, the garden burst
with dandelion seeds
that floated through the doors and cursed
their now transparent need.

Your word checks wayward departures
and puts us to the plow
of Christ your son, and so secures
the gentle snake and cow.

My weight, my love. I love my grave—
I carved a carriage there,
and the wheels in the stone will stay in place
when I will go nowhere.

No man nor angel for angel or man
can spread the seed you plant,
my God. Take up this book of mine—
is not your want its want?

Bishop's Island

For T

1.
We come alive in sea grass here, involve
our hair with cliffs. The horses pastured near
the shrine regard all sentiment with doubt.
A miracle is only what you make,
they whinny, glistening under cloudy light.
An island is only the end of a line that turns
around to know itself.

And islands broken off from islands? What
they know is smaller but the same. So she
and I go look for Bishop's Island, which, so
the story goes (since stories never stay),
became an island when two men came to pray,
prostrate upon the cliffs of their country's edge,
that God would spirit them from the tainted land
whose sins they could no longer bear to tread.
Was the split a surprise

or one of those holy *of courses,* when
the earth tore loose beneath their feet and sailed
not very far away? A monolith
to call their own, and vittles of gull shit
and weeds and glories to God to live on,

and any mackerel the angels dropped.
Two huts of crumbling rock and one gravestone
remain on the grassy top.

Some congratulating bishop named it so.
We lie on the severed edge of the mainland,
and graze our eyes on crests of waves on waves,
intently staring as if an idea
or a dolphin might surface through the spell.
The harps of light unravel consciousness
until we hear a motor, the manure truck
arriving to fertilize the meadow.
We cut away from the cliffs, as slowly as
our wellies carry us.

2.
The story goes that before they were saints
Mael blessed Brigid a bishop by mistake,
if it's a mistake when a tipsy bishop
confuses which consecration rites
are which, and grants a woman the most power
a woman ever wielded in the Church,
and which the Church could not rescind, hiccup!
She promised to pretend, and not to feel "the fullness
of her powers at the precise moment
when she must not use them."

How feminine I feel walking this land,
the wind-combed hair of cliff grass, ocean air
pinking my cheeks, the verdure underfoot
emanating a crisp soft ache for sex
and babies, with a glass-enshrined Mary
in every parish. Very feminine
to listen to the men we meet, gossiping
over absent neighbors, the Dublin bank heist,
"the perpetrators being six people
and one woman." Hiccup.

On the Shannon bus we passed through Kilrush
with Scattery Island on the horizon
and rumors still among its ruins, the tomb
of a nun come to a monastic isle
which St. Sinon insisted no women could
but touch a toe to: the Siren's island
vice versa, and revered. How masculine
we act; we order beers by pints, not halves.
"You're grand, you're grand, you're grand, where are you from?"
To bum a cigarette is dodgy business.
Under the awning by the horseshoe bay,
a man who can't stand except to sing stands
and sings to bend the bow, "The Ballad
of the Ohio River Valley"—where he's
never been but wants to.

3.
There was a pub beside the hillside shrine
and holy well of St. Brigid, and the name
of the pub was Murphy's. We arrived by night,
the arrows and symbols of county roads
and estuarial twilight saw us there.
The glow of lamps faded against the walls
of the unlit shrine, whose archway opened
into turf-black shadows, the well's water
audible at its invisible end,
the doorframe flanked by evidence of prayers
(themselves still sensible in the humid air):
statuettes of the saint piled on her selves,
this one harsher, that one lovelier;
prayer cards and ribbons; rosaries I have
forgotten how to say.

Without a pause my friend walked into the dark,
towards trickling ripples, she the pilgrim soul
whose bravery meets her grace and soothes the saints
that don't need soothing. Her voice traveled behind,
a palm frond she gave me to hold, that I might
follow her. I stayed outside,
within the little light.

They say an ancient eel lives in Brigid's well
and shows himself to those whose prayers she'll grant;
only he knows the eyes that have seen his.
A hidden holy eel nests in the breast,

a creature who, not himself the reason,
knows the reasons I stood at the threshold,
on the reticent side of chill flagstone;
knows the distance between the admittance
of day and subterfuge of night; knows me.
Not so much a blasphemy

to take a picture, to meanly clarify
the dark, as much as a surrendering,
an anti-miracle, as bright and fast
as supplicants wish their pleas could warrant
immediate celestial feats. Like those
two men who sought removal, and received.
Ask God to perform and he'll say, "I am."
Were they prepared to ride the cliffs away,
the results of their Lord and lottery?
After the terrific rock-ripped heave,
when they saw the mainland and no way back,
and when I, to the shudder of an eel,
held the camera inside the shrine and snapped,
were we the same—forever separate
from what we feared, denied, and then desired?

"My Labor, and My Leisure Too" takes its title from Emily Dickinson's "Because I Could Not Stop for Death," and quotes Tom Petty's song, "Walls."

The translations of selected choral odes from Euripides' *Helen* and *Iphigenia in Tauris* in "Mississippi Stasimon" are my own, as are the translations of Apollonius and Propertius in the epigraphs to "The Natural Look" and "Medea in Red River Gorge."

"Myrmidons" is after Ovid's *Metamorphoses*, Book VII: 494-660.

"Last Take" refers to the final scene in *Breakfast at Tiffany's,* where Audrey Hepburn's character emerges from a taxi cab into the rain already drenched—after multiple takes, apparently.

Section Two takes its epigraph from *Albert Camus: A Life* by Olivier Todd, translated by Benjamin Ivry, Knopf Doubleday, 1998.

"The Buried in Sleep and Wine Hotel" takes its title from *Aeneid* II: 265, describing the city of Troy on the night of its destruction as *"somno vinoque sepultam."*

The titles of two poems in the "Hotels, Motels, and Extended Stays" sequence refer to the country songs "Dropkick Me, Jesus" (Paul Craft) and "As Good as I Once Was" (Toby Keith and Scotty Emerick).

"The River of No Return Motel" recommends listening to Marilyn Monroe sing "The River of No Return."

"Si Quaeris Peninsulam Amoenam Circumspice" (if you seek a pleasant peninsula, just look around) is the state motto of Michigan.

"Augustine I – XIII" relates Saint Augustine's *Confessions* in thirteen poems, one for each original book of prose.

"Highway 101" quotes Bob Dylan's song "Spirit on the Water."

"On the Heat of Upstate Travel in the Advancing Polar Air" refers to the Amstutz Expressway, a 2.8-mile stretch of highway in Waukegan, IL. Intended to connect to other major roads, it has not been worked on for decades and has been called "The Road to Nowhere."

The second section of "Bishop's Island" quotes Adrienne Rich's "I Dream I Am the Death of Orpheus."

Katie Hartsock was born in Youngstown, Ohio, and has lived in Cincinnati, Ann Arbor, and Chicago. She holds an MFA from the University of Michigan and a PhD in Comparative Literary Studies from Northwestern University. Recipient of the 2015 Page Davidson Clayton  Prize for Emerging Poets, she is the author of two poetry chapbooks, *Hotels, Motels, and Extended Stays* (Toadlily Press, 2014), and *Veritas Caput* (Passim Editions, 2015). Her poems have appeared in *Beloit Poetry Journal, Massachusetts Review, Southwest Review, RHINO, Measure, Michigan Quarterly Review,* and *Midwestern Gothic,* among other journals, and in the anthology *Down to the Dark River: Poems about the Mississippi River* (Louisiana Literature Press, 2015). She is an assistant professor of English at Oakland University (MI).

ALSO FROM ABLE MUSE PRESS

William Baer, *Times Square and Other Stories*

Melissa Balmain, *Walking in on People – Poems*

Ben Berman, *Strange Borderlands – Poems*

Ben Berman, *Figuring in the Figure – Poems*

Michael Cantor, *Life in the Second Circle – Poems*

Catherine Chandler, *Lines of Flight – Poems*

William Conelly, *Uncontested Grounds – Poems*

Maryann Corbett,
Credo for the Checkout Line in Winter – Poems

John Philip Drury, *Sea Level Rising – Poems*

D.R. Goodman, *Greed: A Confession – Poems*

Margaret Ann Griffiths,
Grasshopper – The Poetry of M A Griffiths

Elise Hempel, *Second Rain – Poems*

Jan D. Hodge, *Taking Shape – carmina figurata*

Ellen Kaufman, *House Music – Poems*

Emily Leithauser, *The Borrowed World – Poems*

Carol Light, *Heaven from Steam – Poems*

April Lindner, *This Bed Our Bodies Shaped – Poems*

Martin McGovern, *Bad Fame – Poems*

Jeredith Merrin, *Cup – Poems*

Richard Newman,
All the Wasted Beauty of the World – Poems

Alfred Nicol, *Animal Psalms – Poems*

Frank Osen, *Virtue, Big as Sin – Poems*

Alexander Pepple (Editor), *Able Muse Anthology*

Alexander Pepple (Editor),
Able Muse – a review of poetry, prose & art
(semiannual issues, Winter 2010 onward)

James Pollock, *Sailing to Babylon – Poems*

Aaron Poochigian, *The Cosmic Purr – Poems*

John Ridland,
Sir Gawain and the Green Knight – Translation

Stephen Scaer, *Pumpkin Chucking – Poems*

Hollis Seamon, *Corporeality – Stories*

Carrie Shipers, *Embarking on Catastrophe – Poems*

Matthew Buckley Smith,
Dirge for an Imaginary World – Poems

Barbara Ellen Sorensen,
Compositions of the Dead Playing Flutes – Poems

Wendy Videlock, *Slingshots and Love Plums – Poems*

Wendy Videlock, *The Dark Gnu and Other Poems*

Wendy Videlock, *Nevertheless – Poems*

Richard Wakefield, *A Vertical Mile – Poems*

Gail White, *Asperity Street – Poems*

Chelsea Woodard, *Vellum – Poems*

www.ablemusepress.com

CPSIA information can be obtained
at www.ICGtesting.com
Printed in the USA
BVHW031957151121
621713BV00004B/296